The Gift of PROPHECY

By Kenneth E. Hagin

Second Edition
First Printing 1986

ISBN 0-89276-015-X

In the U.S. write:
Kenneth Hagin Ministries
P.O. Box 50126
Tulsa, OK 74150-0126

In Canada write:
Kenneth Hagin Ministries
P.O. Box 335
Islington (Toronto), Ontario
Canada, M9A 4X3

Contents

Chapter 1
The Gift of Prophecy in the New Testament Church

Now there are diversities of gifts, but the same Spirit.

And there are differences of administrations, but the same Lord.

And there are diversities of operations, but it is the same God which worketh all in all.

But the manifestation of the Spirit is given to every man to profit withal.

For to one is given by the Spirit the word of wisdom; to another the word of knowledge by the same Spirit;

To another faith by the same Spirit; to another the gifts of healing by the same Spirit;

To another the working of miracles; to another prophecy; to another discerning of spirits; to another divers kinds of tongues; to another the interpretation of tongues.

— 1 Corinthians 12:4-10

Follow after charity, and desire spiritual gifts, but rather that ye may prophesy. . . .

But he that prophesieth speaketh unto men to edification, and exhortation, and comfort. . . .

I would that ye all spake with tongues, but rather that ye prophesied: for greater is he that prophesieth than he that speaketh with tongues, except he interpret, that the church may receive edifying. . . .

Wherefore, brethren, covet to prophesy, and forbid not to speak with tongues.

Let all things be done decently and in order.

— 1 Corinthians 14:1,3,5,39,40

Among the nine gifts of the Spirit there are three *gifts of revelation*, or gifts that reveal something: the word of wisdom, the word of knowledge, and the gift of discern-

1

ing of spirits.

There also are three *power gifts,* or gifts that do something: the gift of faith, working of miracles, and gifts of healings.

Then there are three *gifts of inspiration* — gifts that say something — gifts of utterance: prophecy, divers kinds of tongues, and interpretation of tongues.

The Scriptures stress that the gift of prophecy is the most important gift. Paul said, under the inspiration of the Holy Spirit, *"Greater is he that prophesieth than he that speaketh with tongues"* (1 Cor. 14:5). So prophecy would have to be greater than tongues, "except he interpret."

Paul is saying that tongues with interpretation would be the equivalent of prophecy. Actually, tongues with interpretation *is* prophecy, because prophecy is inspired utterance.

Tongues is inspired utterance in an unknown tongue. *Prophecy* is inspired utterance in a known tongue.

Interpretation of tongues is inspired utterance in your own tongue to give forth that which was said in tongues.

These are all related; all are inspired utterance in its varied forms. In this book, however, we will deal with the specific gift of prophecy.

The gift of prophecy often is confused with the prophetic office. There is the ministry of the prophet, but *not everyone who prophesies is a prophet!*

A rich man has money. Although I may have some money in my wallet, that does not make me a rich man. You may prophesy, but operating the simple gift of prophecy does not qualify you to stand in the office of a prophet.

Naturally, a prophet would have this gift of prophecy in operation, but he also has some of the gifts of revelation. To stand in the office of a prophet, one must have a consistent manifestation of at least two of the revelation gifts (word of wisdom, word of knowledge, or discerning of spirits) plus prophecy.

The office of the prophet is a ministry, a calling. Everyone does not have the same calling and ministry. The Word of God tells us in First Corinthians 12:28, *"And God hath set some in the church, first apostles, secondarily prophets, thirdly teachers. . . ."* Ephesians 4:11 says, speaking of Christ's ascension, *"And he gave some, apostles; and some, prophets; and some, evangelists; and some, pastors and teachers."*

Paul asked the question in First Corinthians 12:29, "Are all apostles?" Of course, the answer is no. Everyone does not have that calling, nor could everyone stand in that office. Then Paul asked, "Are all prophets?" And, of course, the answer is no. Then he asked, "Are all teachers?" (We also could ask, "Are all pastors or evangelists?") We all can witness for Christ, but all of us do not have a calling to the fivefold ministry.*

We can see that the prophetic gift is different from the office of prophet because Paul encouraged the whole Church at Corinth to covet to prophesy. He tells them to *"desire spiritual gifts, but rather that ye may prophesy"* (1 Cor. 14:1). He already had stated in the 12th chapter of First Corinthians that God had set these different ministries in the Church, so he's not telling everyone to seek *the office of prophet.* Instead, he's telling them that all may *prophesy.*

In the 21st chapter of Acts, Luke records that Paul and his company went down to Caesarea and entered the house of Philip the evangelist. The Scriptures tell us that Philip had four daughters who prophesied. It does not call them prophetesses.

When Agabus the prophet came down later, he took Paul's girdle, bound his own hands and feet with it, and said, *"Thus saith the Holy Ghost, So shall the Jews at*

Jerusalem bind the man that owneth this girdle, and shall deliver him into the hands of the Gentiles" (Acts 21:11).

It is one thing to stand in the office of a prophet and it is another thing simply to prophesy. If God calls us to the ministry of a prophet — or any other ministry — He will equip us by the Spirit with the necessary gifts to stand in that office. And men in the Body of Christ shall know you are called and equipped.

If others who have the Spirit do not know you are called and equipped with these gifts, take no offense when they don't accept what you say. Rather, humble yourself before your brethren and take a lesser place. If the Lord sees fit to exalt you, He will exalt you. Then you will have praise of both God and man.

It would be easy to say, "I am a prophet." It would be easy to imitate someone else's ministry. It is another thing entirely to be equipped and called of God. Those who are not called or who only imitate others' ministries are obnoxious to the brethren and they can cause confusion — even division — in the Body of Christ.

The gift of prophecy often is confused with prediction. People think "prophecy" means to predict what will happen in the future. Actually, *the simple gift of prophecy carries no prediction with it whatsoever.* As we read earlier, *". . .he that prophesieth speaketh unto men to EDIFICA-TION, and EXHORTATION, and COMFORT"* (1 Cor. 14:3). Notice that prediction is not mentioned.

Someone may ask, "But wasn't Agabus predicting what would happen to Paul?" Yes, but he wasn't prophesying. Although a prophet may prophesy what is revealed, Agabus was simply telling what the Holy Spirit had told him. Agabus said, *"Thus saith the Holy Ghost. . . ."*

The gift of prophecy also is confused with preaching. Certain denominations teach that preaching is all there is to prophecy. However, the words "preach" and "proph-esy" come from two entirely different Greek words.

To preach means "to proclaim, to announce, to cry, to tell." Jesus said, *"Go ye into all the world, and PREACH the gospel..."* (Mark 16:15). He didn't say to prophesy the Gospel.

Likewise, Paul did not say that men will be saved "by the foolishness of prophesying." He said they will be saved *"by the foolishness of PREACHING"* (1 Cor. 1:21).

The preacher is to *preach* the Word. Paul told Timothy, *"Study to shew thyself approved unto God..."* (2 Tim. 2:15).

So the preacher, the pastor, and the evangelist need to study. If preaching always were prophecy, the preacher would not need to study; he always would speak entirely by inspiration.

There is, however, an element of prophecy in preaching when the preacher becomes so inspired by the Holy Spirit that he says things he normally wouldn't think of. The Holy Spirit inspires him to say it and it is supernatural utterance.

There also is an element of prophecy sometimes in witnessing. I have heard people say, "I began to witness and I spoke Scriptures I had never thought of and didn't even know I knew. I found myself saying things that didn't come out of my head."

That was the spirit of prophecy on them in a measure to speak to a certain person. (Prophecy is a supernatural utterance in a known tongue.) They were speaking super-naturally — beyond the natural.

*For a detailed study of the fivefold ministry gifts, see Rev. Kenneth E. Hagin's study guide entitled *The Ministry Gifts.*

Chapter 2
Prophecy in the Old Testament

In the beginning, God came down and talked to Adam in the Garden of Eden. Through the ages, there has been a longing in the heart of man for a return to this direct communication with his Creator. Through the gift of prophecy we come close to direct communication with Him. It is a gift God has provided primarily for that purpose.

Old and New Testament prophecies differ. Old Testament prophecy essentially is *foretelling*, whereas New Testament prophecy essentially is *forthtelling*.

First Corinthians 14:3 says, *"But he that prophesieth speaketh unto men to edification, and exhortation, and comfort."* That is not foretelling; that is <u>forthtelling</u>.

Old Testament prophecy dealt mostly with the future, sometimes projecting into centuries to come. New Testament prophecy is not so much telling what is going to happen in the future, but it is a ministry to make people better and more useful Christians now.

There are various kinds of prophecies in the Bible. The first mentioned were the *prophecies of the patriarchs* of old. For example, when it came time for Jacob to die, he gathered his children around him, laid hands upon them, and told them things that would happen in the future.

Genesis 49:1 says, *"And Jacob called unto his sons, and said, Gather yourselves together, that I may tell you that which shall befall you in the last days."* Reading further in the chapter, we see that Jacob spoke of events that were to occur centuries in the future. This kind of prophecy was one of foretelling, and it was exercised by faith and by laying on of hands.

Exhortation is another type of prophecy found in the Old Testament. For example, Moses in Deuteronomy told of blessings that would come upon the people for their obedience to God and curses that would come upon them for disobedience.

Prophecy in the Old Testament also takes the form of *songs* or *poetry,* as recorded in the Psalms. The prayers and songs of those inspired writers were given by the spirit of prophecy when they were going through some trial. Today, when we have a similar trial, we can be blessed and inspired by reading how the Spirit of God ministered to them.

Paul, writing to the Church at Ephesus, said, "*. . .be filled with the Spirit; Speaking to yourselves in psalms and hymns and spiritual songs, singing and making melody in your heart to the Lord*" (Eph. 5:18,19). How much more could we be encouraged in tests and trials by speaking to ourselves in psalms.

Some people think that when you talk to yourself, something is wrong with you. I remember a conversation I had once with a friend who said, "My father-in-law is over 80 and his memory has gotten bad due to hardening of the arteries. Sometimes he talks to himself.

"Once when I was helping him with some repairs, he was working on one side of the house and I was on the other. When I finished my side, I walked around to his side and found him talking up a storm — to himself. I asked, 'Pa, who were you talking to?' He smiled and said, 'Well, at least I was talking to a gentleman.'"

At times it's all right to talk to yourself. There were times when David talked to himself under the anointing of the Spirit. David encouraged himself in the Lord. Like David, we also can talk to ourselves in psalms.

A psalm is a spiritual poem or ode. It has an element of poetry to it. It may or may not rhyme. It can be recited or chanted.

Hymns and spiritual songs are meant to be sung.

I speak in psalms because I'm not much of a singer.

(Those who are given to singing probably would sing more.)

Speaking in psalms is in the spirit of prophecy and fills the same purpose: to comfort, exhort, and edify us. Many times in my own life I have been helped immeasurably as I have spoken to myself in psalms hour after hour in the night as the Spirit gave inspiration. These psalms didn't come out of my head; they flowed out of my spirit in direct communication with God. By this method God speaks to us and we converse with Him.

In First Corinthians 14:26 Paul said, *"How is it then, brethren? when ye come together, every one of you hath a psalm...."* They had a psalm because they got a psalm when they were speaking to themselves in psalms at home, praying in the Spirit. *"... every one of you hath a psalm, hath a doctrine, hath a tongue, hath a revelation, hath an interpretation. Let all things be done unto edifying."*

Then in Colossians 3:16 Paul said, *"Let the word of Christ dwell in you richly in all wisdom; teaching and admonishing one another in psalms and hymns and spiritual songs, singing with grace in your hearts to the Lord."*

Thus, through this gift of prophecy, we can sing supernaturally. We can pray supernaturally. We can speak to ourselves through the spirit of prophecy. And we can make intercession for others with this spiritual gift.

Intercession, however, differs from ordinary prayer because it is under the unction of the Holy Spirit. It does not originate in our minds. Our own thinking has nothing to do with it. I have prayed this way for an hour or more and it seemed as if I were kneeling beside myself, listening to myself pray. My mind didn't have a thing to do with it; it just came rolling out of my spirit.

We are exhorted to covet this inspirational gift of prophecy. Under the anointing of the prophetic gift, one may be speaking directly to God, pouring out his deepest devotion. He may be rejoicing before the Lord, magnifying the mercy which God has abundantly bestowed, or he may be glorying in a deliverance. Or, in the Spirit, he may be grieving over the hardness of men's hearts with a grief and deep solemnity which heaven alone can inspire.

Yet another type of prophecy mentioned in the Old Testament is the *prophecy of judgment*. There are conditional prophecies and unconditional prophecies.

The story of King Hezekiah's sickness is an example of a conditional prophecy.

In Second Kings 20:1-3 we read, *"In those days was Hezekiah sick unto death. And the prophet Isaiah. . .said unto him, Thus saith the Lord, Set thine house in order; for thou shalt die, and not live. Then he turned his face to the wall, and prayed unto the Lord, saying, I beseech thee, O Lord, remember now how I have walked before thee in truth and with a perfect heart, and have done that which is good in thy sight. And Hezekiah wept sore."*

Notice Hezekiah said he walked before the Lord with a perfect heart. God is more interested in our having a perfect heart than in our always having perfect actions.

We read further in this chapter, *". . .the word of the Lord came to him* [Isaiah], *saying, Turn again, and tell Hezekiah the captain of my people, Thus saith the Lord, the God of David thy father, I have heard thy prayer, I have seen thy tears: behold, I will heal thee: on the third day thou shalt go up unto the house of the Lord. And I will add unto thy days fifteen years. . ."* (vv. 4-6).

God told Hezekiah that under the present circumstances — if things continued as they were — he should set his house in order, because he was going to die. But the king changed this prophecy. Nobody changed it for him; he changed it for himself. The Bible says he turned his face to the wall, wept, and prayed. Then God sent further word through the prophet, saying, "I have heard your prayer. I'm going to heal you and give you fifteen more years.''

There also were conditional prophecies of blessings in the Old Testament. God spoke through Moses, saying, *"And it shall come to pass, if thou shalt hearken diligently unto the voice of the Lord thy God, to observe and to do all his commandments which I command thee this day, that the Lord thy God will set thee on high above all nations of the earth: And all these blessings shall come on thee, and overtake thee. . .But it shall come to pass, if thou wilt not hearken unto the voice of the Lord thy God, to observe to do all his commandments and his statutes which I command thee this day; that all these curses shall come upon thee, and overtake thee"* (Deut. 28:1,2,15).

I have seen examples of conditional prophecies today. God has tried to encourage His people individually or collectively through prophecy that certain blessings would come upon them or that certain things would happen to them. Often, however, people have fastened their minds on just one part of a prophecy with the attitude, "God said it. Now I'll just see if it comes to pass." There was no faith or action on their part. Later they said, "It hasn't come to pass yet, so it must not have been of God."

We have a part to play in seeing conditional prophecies come to pass. Yes, God has promised us blessings, but it is up to us to keep ourselves under God's flow of blessings and in His will. The fulfillment of conditional prophecy, whether for blessing or judgment, is the responsibility of the individual.

Chapter 3
The Purpose of Prophecy

But he that prophesieth speaketh unto men to edification, and exhortation, and comfort.

— 1 Corinthians 14:3

Let's look in the Bible for scriptural purposes and uses of the gift of prophecy.

First, prophecy is for speaking to men supernaturally: *"He that prophesieth speaketh unto men."* It is supernatural utterance.

Second, it is given to edify the Church: *"He that speaketh in an unknown tongue edifieth himself; but he that prophesieth edifieth the church"* (1 Cor. 14:4).

If one speaks in tongues publicly and interprets it, the Church is edified, because the congregation knows what the speaker has said. If I speak in tongues, it would edify me, but it would not edify others present, because they would not know what was said. But if I interpret, others would be edified.

Greek scholars tell us we have a word in our vernacular today that is closer to the original Greek than the word "edify." "Edify" means "to build up." Greek scholars say the word "charge," as we use it in connection with charging a battery, is a closer translation.

"He that speaketh in an unknown tongue edifieth himself." He builds himself up. He "charges" himself like a battery. Thus, we see the necessity for Spirit-filled believers to pray much in tongues in their private prayer life. It edifies them. It charges them. It builds them up spiritually. Then, when we come together as a body, we are coming together to be edified: *"He that prophesieth edifieth the church."*

Thus, prophecy is given to edify the Church; to build it up spiritually; to charge the Church with spiritual power like a battery.

Another scriptural use of the gift of prophecy is to exhort the Church. The Greek word translated "exhort" here means "a calling near." *"He that prophesieth speaketh unto men to edification* [to build them up, to charge them spiritually], *and exhortation* [a calling near], *and comfort."*

Yet another scriptural use of this gift is to comfort. *God wants to comfort us!* Many people have the wrong mental image of God. They imagine Him as a policeman just waiting to blow the whistle. Others picture God as an austere judge who is just waiting to "throw the book" at them.

The Bible says that God is love (1 John 4:8). If you want to see God, look at Jesus (John 14:9). If you want to know what God is like, see what Jesus is like, because Jesus is God manifested in the flesh.

Jesus said, *"Him that cometh to me I will in no wise cast out"* (John 6:37). He said, *"For the Son of man is come to seek and to save that which was lost"* (Luke 19:10). Jesus also said, *"They that be whole need not a physician, but they that are sick"* (Matt. 9:12).

Someone may say, "But So-and-so is terribly wicked." He needs a "physician" all the more. Like one who is sick, if he doesn't see the Great Physician, he will die. No one would call a doctor to come because someone was well. It is the sick who need help. *God wants to comfort His children.* He wants to call them near.

Some people who supposedly speak by prophetic utterance never speak *comfort* to the Church, however. They never *edify* or *build up* the Church — they give only scathing denunciations. That is *not* the gift of prophecy in operation.

During a seminar I held once in Arizona, I sensed that a fellow sitting near the front had a wrong spirit and he was going to interrupt the service if he could.

Sure enough, when I would stop for a second to catch my breath, he would jump to his feet and yell at the top of his voice.

Some people think they can convince others they are anointed if they display some kind of physical manifestation. They think if they jump, jerk, yell, or talk in a falsetto voice, people will think they really have spiritual power. "The Holy Ghost made me do that," they will say. The Holy Spirit doesn't work that way, because we see in First Corinthians 14:32, *"The spirits of the prophets are subject to the prophets."*

When this fellow yelled, I stopped teaching. His behavior was most unedifying. It seemed as if someone had poured a bucket of cold water over the congregation. As soon as he stopped, I started talking as fast as I could to bring my message to a conclusion.

The next night, the fellow returned. I decided that if he performed again, I would have to give some instruction to the congregation, letting them know (without embarrassing the man) that this wasn't right.

While teaching, I tried to talk as hard and fast as I could, not giving him a place to break in. He finally jumped to his feet, however, and took off anyway. Again it was most unedifying.

I mentioned that if we felt God was trying to use us, we should be careful not to interrupt someone who was speaking. The Holy Spirit is a gentleman, I explained. If I am anointed by the Holy Spirit and the other person is anointed by the Holy Spirit, the Holy Spirit would be interrupting Himself.

Hearing this, the fellow became angry. He didn't come back for three nights. I had been speaking about ten minutes that third night when he leaped to his feet and said, "I'm going to give you one more chance. If you don't repent, the whole group is going to hell." He went on and on and finally wound up by saying, "This is your last chance."

I went on teaching as if nothing had happened, so he stomped out of the meeting. He was not in the Spirit. That was not the gift of prophecy.

People like him probably do receive something from God to begin with, but they are immature Christians. It is as if they got a little red wagon for Christmas and all they want to do is pull it back and forth in front of their house so everyone can see it.

First Corinthians 14:32 says, *"The spirits of the prophets are subject to the prophets."* This means you have the power to keep quiet or to talk. *The Amplified Bible* says, "For the spirits of the prophets [the speakers in tongues] are under the speaker's control [and subject to being silenced as may be necessary]." Verse 40 says, *"Let all things be done decently and in order."* Remember, the Holy Spirit is not going to interrupt Himself!

In First Corinthians 14, Paul tells us that the gift of prophecy also is able to convict the unbeliever and to make manifest the secrets of his heart:

> 1 CORINTHIANS 14:23-25
> 23 If therefore the whole church be come together into one place, and all speak with tongues, and there come in those that are unlearned, or unbelievers, will they not say that ye are mad?
> 24 But if all prophesy, and there come in one that believeth not, or one unlearned, he is convinced of all, he is judged of all:
> 25 And thus are the secrets of his heart made manifest; and so falling down on his face he will worship God, and report that God is in you of a truth.

Once while I was preaching in Texas, this spirit of prophecy moved upon me just after I had preached my sermon. The church was full. I found myself pointing to a stranger in the back of the building. I said, "Stand to your feet and step out in the aisle." This long, tall Texan stepped out. The thought then crossed my mind, *Dear Lord, what am I going to do now?*

I heard myself telling him, "Before you came to church tonight, you said to your wife. . . ." I told him exactly what he had said to his wife earlier. He was unsaved. He had said some things to her about God and salvation and what he never would do.

Before I stopped talking, he suddenly ran down the aisle and fell on his knees at the altar with his hands raised. He gave his heart to Jesus and started talking in tongues almost immediately.

He told me afterwards, "You must have known the secrets of my heart, because I said that very thing."

Chapter 4
The Difference Between Prophecy and Interpretation of Tongues

In studying prophecy, we need to note the difference between interpretation of tongues and prophecy. The Bible says, *"... greater is he that prophesieth than he that speaketh with tongues"* (1 Cor. 14:5), although both are inspired utterances.

Tongues, of course, is inspired utterance in an *unknown* tongue. The interpretation of tongues is inspired utterance telling that which was spoken in tongues.

Prophecy is inspired utterance in a *known* tongue. The difference between interpretation and prophecy is that interpretation is dependent upon tongues, whereas prophecy isn't.

There can be no interpretation without tongues. And then it is *interpretation* of tongues, not "translation" of tongues. For that reason, the message in tongues may be long and the interpretation short because the interpretation only gives the meaning. Or one may speak a short time in tongues and then give a lengthy interpretation. There also are times when the interpretation may be almost word for word. I have experienced this. I have spoken in a language not known to me, but known to someone in the congregation. Afterwards they said I gave the meaning almost word for word.

The New Testament emphasizes the *exhortational* kind of prophecy rather than prophecy of *revelation.* First Corinthians 14:3 says, *"But he that prophesieth speaketh unto men to edification, and exhortation, and comfort."* The New Testament does speak of the revelation kind of prophecy, but it is not emphasized. The exhortational kind is the most needful in the congregation. The revelation kind of prophecy may be demonstrated occasionally, but usually it would be manifested through a prophet rather than through one who just prophesies or through the gift of prophecy alone.

Paul teaches concerning revelation prophecy: *"Let the prophets speak two or three, and let the other* [prophets] *judge. If any thing be revealed to another that sitteth by, let the first hold his peace. For ye may all prophesy one by one, that all may learn, and all may be comforted"* (1 Cor. 14:29-31). This passage should not be taken out of context and applied to everyone. Paul is referring here to prophets, because in the 32nd verse he says, *"And the spirits of the prophets are subject to the PROPHETS."*

Some have misinterpreted the 26th verse in this chapter — *"when ye come together, every one of you hath a psalm, hath a doctrine, hath a tongue, hath a revelation, hath an interpretation"* — to mean that each person had all these. The Greek word for the phrase "every one of you" is an all-inclusive term meaning "within the whole body."

In other words, some would have a psalm, others a tongue, and still others a revelation. Each would not have the same thing, for there would be no purpose in such duplication. That would be as if I were to ask three people to sing a special song, and each sang the same song.

Some have gotten the idea that when tongues and interpretation or prophecies are given, God actually is speaking. There is a *sense* in which it is God speaking, but if God actually were speaking, we would not have any right to judge it.

Second, if God actually were speaking, we would not need any instructions for the use of the gifts — when to speak and when not to speak — because God does not need any instructions.

The gifts of God are perfect. The Holy Spirit is perfect. But these gifts are not always perfect *in manifestation,* because they are manifested through an imperfect channel: men and women. The Spirit of God flows through us as

water flows through a pipe. Sometimes the Spirit of God
flowing through us picks up something from our own per-
sonality. (After all, God uses personalities.)

God doesn't put a premium on ignorance *or* education,
but He has to use the vessel such as it is. I have seen the
anointing of the Spirit of God upon one who is educated,
cultured, and refined, and I was greatly blessed. On the
other hand, I have heard interpretations of messages which
included such words as "hain't," "ain't," "you'uns," and
"we'uns." Those giving the interpretations could not go
beyond their capacity. They used the best vocabulary they
had. It was the Spirit of God in manifestation, but it was
not a perfect manifestation.

A minister tells that in one of his services the interpretation given of a message in tongues was: "My little
children, don't be scared — that is, if you *are* my little
children. But if you are scared, I don't blame you, because
sometimes I get scared myself."

Although this was not a manifestation of the Spirit of
God, it does not mean that the dear soul who gave it was
not a Christian. It does not even mean that she wasn't
filled with the Holy Spirit. She wanted God to use her,
but she was just speaking out of her own mind.

Many times we let such manifestations scare a lot of
good people off instead of giving people the right teaching.
We need the operation of the gifts in our congregations.
We need everything God has provided, but we need to
follow God's instructions for the proper use of these gifts
so that *"all things be done unto edifying"* (1 Cor. 14:26).

Some excuse their spiritual excesses by saying, "I
couldn't help that. The Holy Spirit made me do it." They
blame the Holy Spirit for their being out of order. But the
Holy Spirit, through Paul, has given us instructions so
we know how to be in order.

Although we may be inspired to speak — we may have

a message in tongues and interpretation, or even a word of prophecy — it is not always wise to jump up at any time. If our inspiration comes at an inopportune moment when it would not be edifying, then we should hold our peace. At the right time we can give what we have.

Many times when attending fellowship meetings and campmeetings where I was not the speaker, I could have spoken with tongues but didn't. The leaders of the meetings were men who knew God, who were filled with the Spirit, and they could give the message themselves. There was no need of my butting in from out in the congregation. In a large gathering if someone speaks in tongues or prophesies from the congregation, few hear it. If it comes from the platform, however, everyone hears it, and it is edifying.

The inspirational and the revelation gifts are a product of both God *and* man. It isn't all God and it isn't all man. This is where many have missed the blessing of being filled with the Spirit. They could have spoken in tongues many years ago.

Many have had the Holy Spirit all along, but they haven't enjoyed His fullness because of mistaken ideas. Some have said to me when I told them this, "If I had known this, I could have talked in tongues 25 years ago. I had an urge to say something that wasn't English, but I thought if I spoke that out, it would just be *me* doing it. I have been waiting for the Holy Spirit to talk with tongues all these years."

However, He doesn't really talk with tongues. Nowhere in the Bible does it say that the Holy Spirit ever talked with tongues. Instead, we read that the Holy Spirit gives *you* utterance, and *you* do the talking. That is what happened on the Day of Pentecost: *"And they were all filled with the Holy Ghost, and* [they] *began to speak with other tongues, as the Spirit gave them utterance"* (Acts 2:4). He gave them the utterance; they did the talking.

After hearing this preached, some people have asked me, "Why didn't someone tell me? I have been afraid to talk in tongues — afraid it would just be the flesh." But when you talk in tongues, it *will* be you *in the flesh.* God said He would pour out His Spirit *on all flesh.* Everyone who ever talked with tongues was in the flesh, but he was inspired by the Spirit.

The same thing is true with the inspirational and revelation gifts of God. They are a product of both man and God.

Prophecy is a result of the merging of the divine and the human.

First Timothy 4:14 says, *"Neglect not the gift that is in thee, which was given thee by prophecy, with the laying on of the hands of the presbytery."* Second Timothy 1:6 says, *"Wherefore I put thee in remembrance that thou stir up the gift of God, which is in thee by the putting on of my hands."* You are responsible for stirring up the gift within you — not God and not the Holy Spirit, although He is the motivating power.

In Full Gospel circles we have a Pentecostal jargon that often blinds us. For instance, some pray, "Pour out your Spirit upon us, Lord. We need an outpouring of the Holy Spirit." Yet we cannot find in the New Testament where the Holy Spirit was ever poured out on a church, where they were ever told to pray for an outpouring, or where the Holy Spirit ever was poured out on Spirit-filled believers.

The Holy Spirit is poured out on people who don't have the Holy Spirit!

The outpouring of the Holy Spirit came on the Jews on the Day of Pentecost. The outpouring of the Holy Spirit came to the Gentiles one day at Cornelius' house. The world may need an outpouring of the Spirit, but the Church doesn't. Believers already have the Spirit. What they need to do is to stir up what they have!

The Church often is sitting around praying for an outpouring, drying up, starving to death, when they already are *thoroughly equipped* with all they need. If they would just stir up what they already have, they would be revived!

We, not the Holy Spirit, are responsible for the use of God's power. Every now and then we have to do exactly what Paul told Timothy to do: "Stir up the gift of God."

Chapter 5
Guidance and the Gift of Prophecy

And now, behold, I go bound in the spirit unto Jerusa-
lem, not knowing the things that shall befall me there:
Save that the Holy Ghost witnesseth in every city,
saying that bonds and afflictions abide me. . . .

[Agabus the prophet] *took Paul's girdle, and bound his*
own hands and feet, and said, Thus saith the Holy Ghost,
So shall the Jews at Jerusalem bind the man that owneth
this girdle, and shall deliver him into the hands of the
Gentiles.

— Acts 20:22,23; 21:11

God has several ways of showing His children His will
for their lives. He speaks through the written Word — the
Bible. He speaks through the preached Word as His
ministers preach the Bible. He guides through controlling
circumstances. And He speaks through the gift of prophecy at times.* This is an area in which great care must
be exercised, however, as some have fallen into error here.
We must be careful to follow scriptural guidelines.

When God spoke to Paul through the prophet Agabus,
as quoted in the above Scripture, the Spirit only told Paul
what was going to happen. It was then up to Paul to
choose whether or not to go.

There has been a trend in recent years for denomina-
tional Christians who have been filled with the Holy Spirit
to gather in one another's homes for prayer meetings.

One woman who regularly attended such meetings
came to me, confused, saying, "In our prayer meetings,
the people spend hours laying hands on one another and
praying and prophesying to one another. Maybe it's all
right, but it seems to me that all of the prophesying is concerning something bad. One time they prophesied that my
mother was going to die, but she hasn't died yet. She isn't

even sick. It seems as if I always get a bad prophecy. It disturbs me."

Often such meetings degenerate into little more than fortune-telling, which is apart from the Spirit of God entirely. The gifts of the Spirit are not to be played with like children's toys. They are to be reverenced. They are to be brought into the open, where they can be judged.

God didn't set prophecy or prophets in Sister Jones' kitchen. He set them in the Church. That does not mean that it would not be all right to prophesy in your kitchen or living room, but it means that we should prophesy primarily in church, where all can judge the prophecies.

I know people who have entered into marriages because someone prophesied they should marry a certain individual; then life became miserable for both of them. The Bible lays down certain rules concerning marriage. We should look to God's Word and ask Him for guidance along these lines.

The gift of prophecy is not to be used to introduce new doctrine. The Bible is our source of doctrine. We should beware of so-called prophets who come with their new doctrines, "deeper truth," "new light," or something else. Usually these people, who are supposed to get some new revelation that no one else has, do much damage to the cause of Christ.

Prophecy is primarily speaking *"unto men to EDIFICATION, and EXHORTATION, and COMFORT"* (1 Cor. 14:3). The Spirit of God is not going to give something that would divide the Church! That is not the spirit of love.

Often these people become filled with pride. Some have told me they are right and everyone else is wrong. They have said, "Unless you believe as I do, you are going to be lost." When asked to give Scripture for their new "revelation," they have replied, "You have to have the revelation. This is *beyond* the Bible."

A minister who at one time was very sound said, "I don't need that book any more. I am beyond it." Then he threw the Bible on the floor, saying, "I have the Holy Spirit. I am a prophet. God sends my instructions direct." It was not long until he was prophesying that people should each give him a hundred dollars. He was getting his instructions direct — but direct from where?

The gift of prophecy is not to settle arguments. The twelfth chapter of Luke records that some people wanted Jesus to settle an argument, but Jesus refused to do so. Arguments should be settled according to the Word of God.

The gift of prophecy is not to be used merely to satisfy curiosity. It is not to be used as a gimmick. There is a vast difference between the gift of prophecy and the prying into the future by fortune-tellers, sorcerers, astrologers, etc. All these things are a counterfeit of the true gift of prophecy.

A true message of prophecy will edify, exhort, and comfort people, helping them to be better Christians.

Some of these mystics and psychic mediums even will predict which horse is going to win which race, or which candidate is going to win a political race. But God is not in that. Remember that the Bible forbids our having anything to do with sorcerers, fortune-tellers, psychic mediums, and the like. The Spirit of God can tell us things if He wishes, but we need to know the difference between the true and the false. If we don't, we had better stay away from any of it until we do.

How can we tell the difference between an operation of the Spirit of God and an extrasensory manifestation? *That which is of God centers around Christ.* It is not something to be used to prove that I have something, or that I am somebody.

Saul once had the Spirit of God, but when he got away from God, an evil spirit came to him. There are people today who once were used of God, but later they began operating under an evil spirit.

A certain minister I know was at one time used of God in the word of knowledge and the revelation gifts. He was visiting a church where I was preaching, and the pastor asked him to say a few words. While he was speaking, the Spirit of God said to me, "He has a familiar spirit."

The minister said, "You think I am not a prophet of God? Why, your name is So-and-so. Your address is such-and-such. You are so many years old, and in your billfold you have so many dollars. Isn't that so?" The person said it was so.

One man had a valuable diamond ring at home. The minister said to him, "You have a valuable diamond ring at home in such-and-such a drawer. God said for you to give it to me." The man knew that this was supernatural. It had to be God, he thought, so he got the ring and gave it to the minister. Charlatans line their pockets this way. But that was not God's power in demonstration; it was a familiar spirit.

Familiar spirits are familiar with you. They know about you and they tell people things about you. By the same token, the Spirit of God could do the same thing through the word of knowledge if He saw fit to do so. But it would not be just a public display for mere curiosity. It would be for your edification, not to attract attention to a man, to cause people to think he is someone great, to line his pockets with money, or to put diamonds or watches in his hand.

The gift of prophecy is real. It is good. It is right. It can be used for good.

*For a detailed study of this subject, see Rev. Kenneth E. Hagin's book *How You Can Be Led by the Spirit of God.*

Chapter 6
Seven Steps To Judging Prophecy

As New Testament Christians we need the operation of the gifts of the Spirit in our churches today. We should encourage every flame of fire that comes from God. But we also should realize that there are both true and false gifts. However, there is no need to be afraid of the gifts of the Spirit just because some false elements have crept in.

Jesus warned against false prophets, saying, *"Beware of false prophets, which come to you in sheep's clothing, but inwardly they are ravening wolves"* (Matt. 7:15). Paul and Peter, writing to the Church in their day, warned against false prophets, false apostles, and false prophecies (2 Cor. 11:13; 2 Peter 2:1). And if such a warning was necessary then, it is necessary now.

How can we recognize false prophets?*

Jesus said, *"Ye shall know them by their fruits. Do men gather grapes of thorns, or figs of thistles? Even so every good tree bringeth forth good fruit; but a corrupt tree bringeth forth evil fruit. A good tree cannot bring forth evil fruit, neither can a corrupt tree bring forth good fruit. . . . Wherefore by their fruits ye shall know them"* (Matt. 7:16-18,20).

A minister who seemingly was mightily used in prophecy was approached about questions that were being raised concerning his ministry. He replied, "There is no truth in that — it's all lies." He later told another group confidentially, "I don't let them know I believe this. It's all right to lie as long as you're lying for good."

It is wrong to lie regardless of the reason! That preacher could prophesy loud and long, but who could believe his prophecies?

So the first step in judging prophecy is, *"By their fruits ye shall know them."*

The second step in judging prophecy is: "Does it glorify Christ?" Jesus, speaking about the Holy Spirit, said, *"He shall glorify me"* (John 16:14).

Let us look at some Scriptures along this line.

Revelation 19:10 *"And I fell at his feet to worship him* [the angel]. *And he said unto me, See thou do it not: I am thy fellowservant, and of thy brethren that have the testimony of Jesus: worship God: for the testimony of Jesus is the spirit of prophecy."* If the prophecy is right, and the prophet is right, they will testify of Jesus. If either attracts attention to man, however, it is wrong, because *"He shall glorify me."*

First Corinthians 12:3: *". . . no man speaking by the Spirit of God calleth Jesus accursed: and that no man can say that Jesus is the Lord, but by the Holy Ghost."* (Paul said in the first verse of this chapter, *"Now concerning spiritual gifts, brethren, I would not have you ignorant."*) He is saying that when spiritual gifts, including prophecy, are in operation, they will make Jesus Lord.

First John 4:1,2: *"Beloved, believe not every spirit, but try the spirits whether they are of God: because many false prophets are gone out into the world. Hereby know ye the Spirit of God: Every spirit that confesseth that Jesus Christ is come in the flesh is of God."*

If the prophecy is of God, it points to Jesus. Therefore, we can judge both prophets and prophecies according to their attitude toward Jesus. If they lead us away from Him, or if they create division in the Body of Christ, they are wrong. If they magnify man rather than Christ, they are wrong.

I have heard prophecies go forth that elevated man and appealed to human and spiritual pride. One such prophecy, given to a zealous young man who wanted to do something for God, said, "Thus saith the Lord: If you will follow me, young man, I will make you the greatest preacher that the world has ever seen. In fact, you will have a ministry that is greater than all the apostles and all the prophets of all ages put together. There is not a minister in America today who will be as great as you."

This prophecy naturally thrilled the young preacher, because he wanted to be someone great and important. But the misguided prophetess was not anointed of the Spirit of God when she spoke such words, because they exalted man, not Christ.

God wants us to be humble before Him. Young and immature Christians sometimes are hurt by such false prophecies. This is why we need sound teaching concerning the gifts of the Spirit.

The third step in judging prophecy is to ask, "Does it agree with the Scriptures?" If it is a true prophecy, it will be according to the Word of God, because *the Spirit and the Word agree.*

The Word of God was inspired by the Holy Spirit. Holy men of old wrote as they were inspired by the Spirit of God. The Holy Spirit is not going to tell you one thing in the Word and another through prophecy. If it doesn't agree with the Word of God, it isn't right!

This does not mean that it is necessarily from the devil. It could be an evil spirit, but sometimes it is just the result of human reasoning. The fact that a person would unknowingly listen to an evil spirit does not mean that he is not a Christian, or even that he is not Spirit filled.

One time when Jesus was talking to His disciples concerning His death on the cross, Peter said, "Not so, Lord." Jesus turned to Peter and said, "Get thee behind me, Satan." Jesus was not calling Peter Satan, but Peter had unknowingly listened to the devil and had repeated the wrong thing.

It is essential that we know the Word of God, because we cannot judge prophecy without a thorough knowledge of God's Word.

The fourth step is to ask, "Are their prophecies fulfilled?" We read in Deuteronomy 18:

DEUTERONOMY 18:20-22
20 But the prophet, which shall presume to speak a word in my name, which I have not commanded him to speak, or that shall speak in the name of other gods, even that prophet shall die.
21 And if thou say in thine heart, How shall we know the word which the Lord hath not spoken?
22 When a prophet speaketh in the name of the Lord, if the thing follow not, nor come to pass, that is the thing which the Lord hath not spoken, but the prophet hath spoken it presumptuously. . . .

There are some who are presumptuous and prophesy out of their own minds. Their prophecies are not fulfilled.

Then again — and this is step number five — we need to realize that some prophecies are not necessarily of God, even though they may come to pass:

DEUTERONOMY 13:1-5
1 If there arise among you a prophet, or a dreamer of dreams, and giveth thee a sign or a wonder,
2 And the sign or the wonder come to pass, whereof he spake unto thee, saying, Let us go after other gods, which thou hast not known, and let us serve them;
3 Thou shalt not hearken unto the words of that prophet, or that dreamer of dreams: for the Lord your God proveth you, to know whether ye love the Lord your God with all your heart and with all your soul.
4 Ye shall walk after the Lord your God, and fear him, and keep his commandments, and obey his voice, and ye shall serve him, and cleave unto him.
5 And that prophet, or that dreamer of dreams, shall be put to death; because he hath spoken to turn you away from the Lord your God. . . .

Sometimes people think, *That must be right. It came to pass.* But even though it came to pass, it was not of God.

How can you tell when something is not of God? Look again at step two: Does this prophecy lead you *to* God or *away from* Him? Does it cause you to become more reverent toward God and the Bible, or does it lead you away from the New Birth and other fundamental doctrines?

Step six is to ask, "Do the prophecies produce liberty or bondage?" Second Corinthians 4:13 says, *"We having the same spirit of faith, according as it is written, I believed, and therefore have I spoken; we also believe, and therefore speak."* If it is in the same spirit of faith that we are in, then it will produce *liberty.* If not, it will produce *bondage.* Many are led into bondage instead of being led into light and deliverance.

In Romans 8:15 we read, *"For ye have not received the spirit of bondage again to fear; but ye have received the Spirit of adoption, whereby we cry, Abba, Father."* God is not going to lead us back into fear. We have been delivered from the spirit of fear!

We find the last step to judging prophecy in First John 2:20,27: *"But ye have an unction from the Holy One, and ye know all things. . . . But the anointing which ye have received of him abideth in you. . . ."* Unction is anointing.

When things are not right, something inside you — an unction of the Lord, the anointing that abides in you — tells you something is wrong. The Holy Spirit is there to inform you if things are not as they should be, and you will know immediately.

Don't let fanaticism and excesses keep you from the blessings of God. You can't fight error with error. Teach the New Testament. Believe in the Spirit of God and the gifts of the Spirit, and enjoy all that God has provided for His children.

---

*For a detailed study of this topic, see Rev. Kenneth E. Hagin's book *Seven Steps for Judging Prophecy.*